Rastamouse
SONGBOOK for UKULELE

ISBN 978-1-4803-5324-4

HAL•LEONARD®
CORPORATION

7777 W. BLUEMOUND RD. P.O. BOX 13819 MILWAUKEE, WI 53213

In Australia Contact:
Hal Leonard Australia Pty. Ltd.
4 Lentara Court
Cheltenham, Victoria, 3192 Australia
Email: ausadmin@halleonard.com.au

® and ™ 2013 – The Rastamouse Company Limited

Visit Hal Leonard Online at
www.halleonard.com

www.rastamouse.com

Best Friends

Music by Andrew Kingslow
Words by Andrew Kingslow and Sara Dowling

Come an' Sing Along Wid Me

Words and Music by Andrew Kingslow

Cookin' & Jammin'

Music by Andrew Kingslow
Words by Andrew Kingslow and Brian Jordan

Pots and pans are all a - bang - in', spoons and forks and knives are clang - in'. All our time we be a - spend - in'

Pre-Chorus

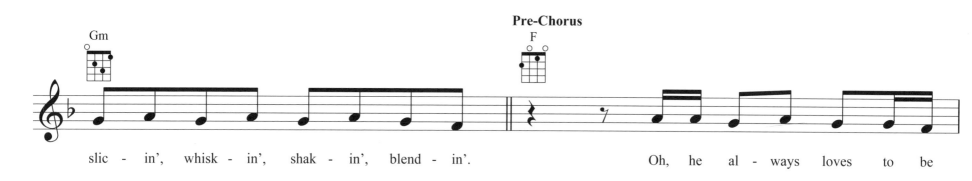

slic - in', whisk - in', shak - in', blend - in'. Oh, he al - ways loves to be

cook - in'. When he's cook - in' in his hat, he's danc - in'. All the pots and pans in the

kitch - en start a - shik - a shak - a shak - in' when he's danc - in'. Oh, he al - ways loves to be

cook - in'. When he's cook - in' in his hat, he's danc - in'. All the pots and pans in the

kitch - en start a - shik - a shak- a shak - in' when he's danc - in'.

Chorus

Cook - in' and jam - min', cook - in' and jam - min', cook - in' and jam - min',

cook - in' and jam - min'. Cook - in' and jam - min'. _____

Da Rhymin' Teef

Words and Music by Andrew Kingslow

Da Sugamice

Words and Music by Andrew Kingslow

We work hard both day and night just to get our mu-sic

groov-in' real tight. There is no sim-ple way to suc-cess,

no mag-ic po-tion that will help you pro-gress un-less you

Chorus

work, work, work, work real hard, un - less you

work, work, work, that's if you wan - na get far, un - less you

work, work, work, you got - ta try, try, try, un - less you

work, _____ that's if you wan - na get a slice of the pie. _____

Everyone's a Winner

Music by Andrew Kingslow
Words by Andrew Kingslow, Genevieve Webster and Michael De Souza

Me name Bag - ga T and me been told *(Instrumental)* to

win da race is da on - ly goal. *(Instrumental)* But

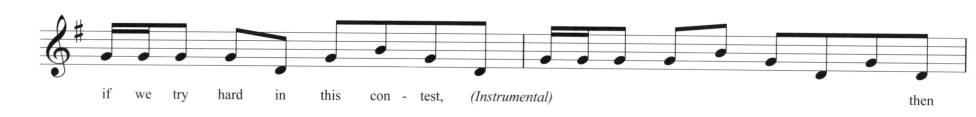

if we try hard in this con - test, *(Instrumental)* then

we know that we done we best. *(Instrumental)*

Chorus

Ev - 'ry - one's a win - ner, you got to give it all your heart, no

mat - ter if you win or lose, just as long as you're tak - ing part.

Life is for da liv - ing, you got to give it all you got, just as

long as you al - ways try your best to reach the num - ber one spot.

Give It Up for Da Easy Crew

(Rastamouse Theme)

Music by Andrew Kingslow
Words by Andrew Kingslow, Martin Merchant, Genevieve Webster and Michael De Souza

First note

Intro
Moderately bright Reggae

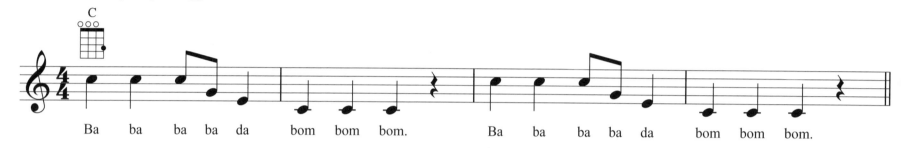

Ba ba ba ba da bom bom bom. Ba ba ba ba da bom bom bom.

Verse

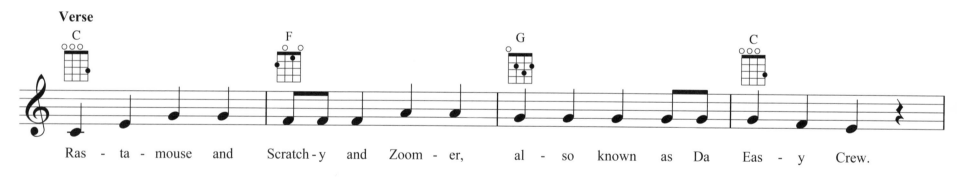

Ras - ta - mouse and Scratch-y and Zoom - er, al - so known as Da Eas - y Crew.

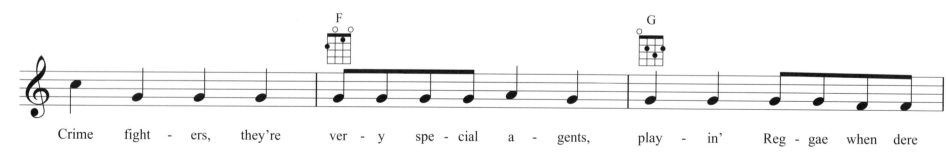

Crime fight - ers, they're ver - y spe - cial a - gents, play - in' Reg - gae when dere

Grovetown

Words and Music by Andrew Kingslow

Grove - town,   oh,   Grove - town.   So   come   a - long   and   sing   with   me.

Chorus

Why   don't   you   come   down   to   my   Grove - town?   We   are   all   fam - i - ly,   we

nev - er   let   you   down.   There's   no   bet - ter   place   to   wear   a   smil - ing   face,   so ____

why   don't   you   come   down   to   my   Grove - town?

Ice Popp

Music by Andrew Kingslow
Words by Andrew Kingslow and Lee Pressman

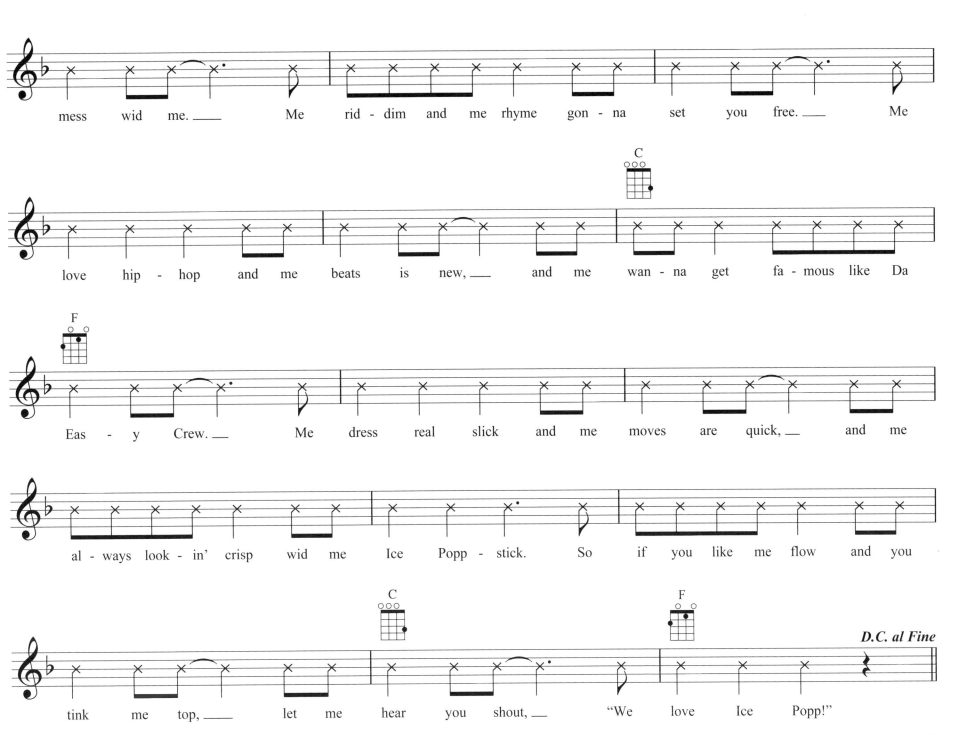

mess wid me.____ Me rid - dim and me rhyme gon - na set you free.____ Me

love hip - hop and me beats is new, ____ and me wan - na get fa - mous like Da

Eas - y Crew. ____ Me dress real slick and me moves are quick, ____ and me

al - ways look - in' crisp wid me Ice Popp - stick. So if you like me flow and you

tink me top, ____ let me hear you shout, ____ "We love Ice Popp!"

D.C. al Fine

Life Is Sweet

Music by Andrew Kingslow
Words by Andrew Kingslow and Andrew Smith

Firstnote

Verse
Moderate Calypso feel

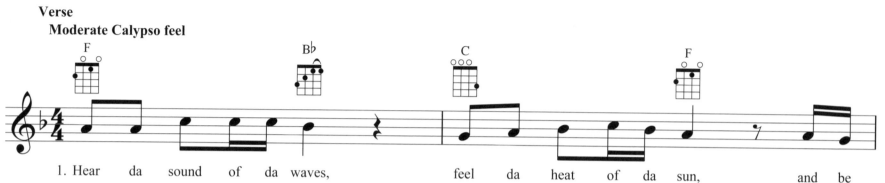

1. Hear da sound of da waves, feel da heat of da sun, and be

hap - py ev - 'ry day of your life for da wick - ed friends that you got.

Verse

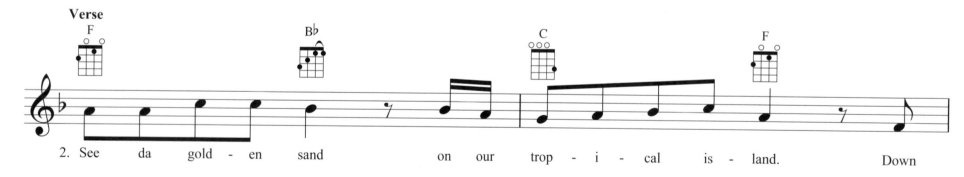

2. See da gold - en sand on our trop - i - cal is - land. Down

on da beach we love to swim in da beau - ti - ful blue sea. Oh, _____

Chorus

life is sweet ___ for ev - 'ry - one. ___ It's oh, so sweet ___ when you're

hav - ing fun. _____ We love to play _____ un - der da

shin - ing sun. ___ Life is sweet ___ for ev - 'ry - one. ___

Originality

Music by Andrew Kingslow
Words by Andrew Kingslow, Genevieve Webster and Michael De Souza

Run Wid Me

Music by Andrew Kingslow
Words by Andrew Kingslow and Sara Dowling

25

Take It Easy

Words and Music by Andrew Kingslow

Ya Never Too Old

Music by Andrew Kingslow
Words by Andrew Kingslow and Lee Pressman

and   ya   nev - er   too   young   to   strum   a   gui - tar.
Ya   nev - er   too   old   to   do   just   what   you   like.

Chorus

We   can   do   an - y - ting,   ting,   ting.   We   just   love

to   sing,   sing,   sing.   All   the   peo - ple   come   and   see   us   sing - ing   in

per - fect   har - mo - ny.

Hot Hot Hot

Words and Music by Andrew Kingslow

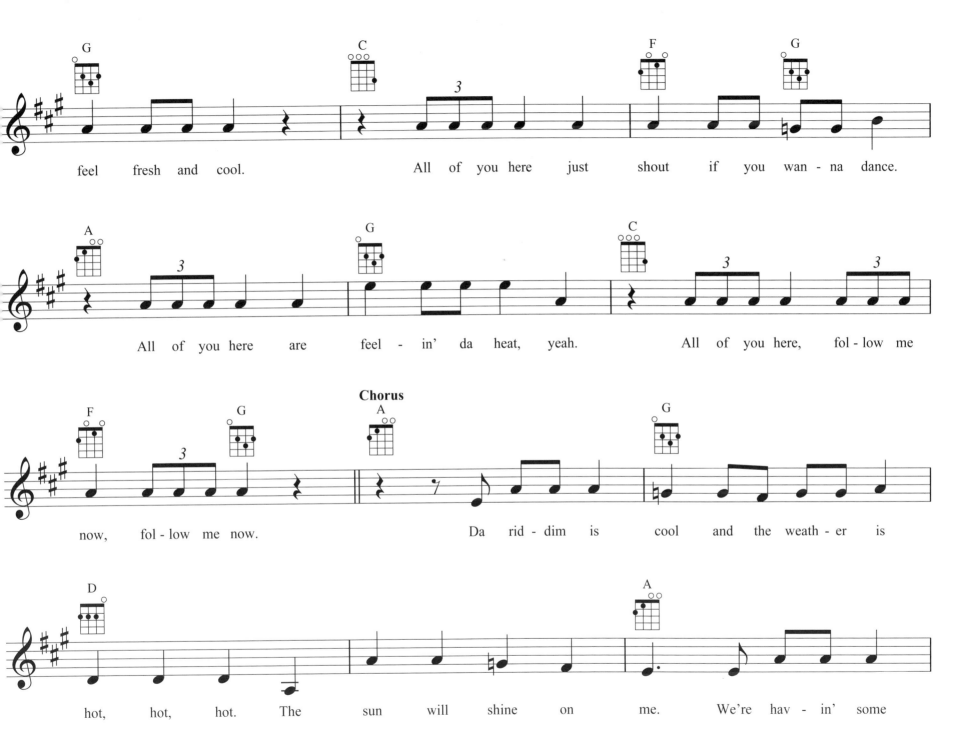

feel   fresh   and   cool.   All   of   you   here   just   shout   if   you   wan - na   dance.

All   of   you   here   are   feel - in'   da   heat,   yeah.   All   of   you   here,   fol - low   me

Chorus

now,   fol - low   me   now.   Da   rid - dim   is   cool   and   the   weath - er   is

hot,   hot,   hot.   The   sun   will   shine   on   me.   We're   hav - in'   some

fun when the weath - er is hot, hot, hot. Get up and move your

feet. _____ Da rid - dim is cool and the weath - er is hot, hot, hot. The

sun will shine on me. We're hav - in' some fun when the weath - er is

hot, hot, hot. Get up and move your feet.